To Tani,
My friend! We
really started from
Bottom. Thank you for
your support!
♡ Halton.

Holly Cotton

STRONG.

MORE THAN

MUSCLES.

A story of surviving cancer, finding purpose

and living life.

NOTE TO READERS:

Holly is grateful to all of her physicians for their excellent care and compassion. Out of respect for the patient/doctor relationship their names have been omitted from the scenarios.

Her stories are written from memories she holds close to her heart.

TABLE OF CONTENTS

PREFACE:

This is my story of being strong. Being a breast cancer survivor. Surviving life. Becoming a whole new person that is the strongest me I could have ever imagined.

Chapter One: The Call

Why do traumatic events always happen in slow motion? It seems like you remember every single detail of the event like it just happened. This is my story...

The day my life changed began as a normal day for me. Background...I was 36 years old and working as a nursing director of an assisted living facility. I thought I had a pretty good life. I have two awesome kids (we all think our kids are the most awesome beings don't we?). I was separated from my husband and trying to figure out how to navigate through life as a single mom. Trying to find my independence. I exercised five to six days a week. I was in pristine shape. I could do pullups and pushups like a pro. Although I was already a nurse, I only had an associate degree. I tried going back to college to complete a bachelor degree nursing program several times in my 20's. Kids, jobs, bills, life in general always got in the way. I was determined from the day my son was born to be the best mom I could be, so those were my priorities. When I applied for college in 2012 I thought, this is it! I am going to accomplish this goal no matter what! I started the nursing program that August. I was ecstatic to go to class. I was on time every day, sat in the front seat with my binder and pencil case like a kindergartener! My schedule was insane during this period. School every morning for four hours followed by me going to work for eight hours. I even worked on weekends. I was determined to do whatever I needed to do to complete the program this time.

October 1, 2012. I got into the shower that evening and for some reason my hand slid over a small mole I had on my left breast. There it was. A lump. It felt like a small marble. I felt it a hundred times. I got out of the shower, felt it again. It was still there. I immediately knew it was cancer. That night I tossed and turned all night. Worried about what was going on. Telling myself not to overreact. It didn't work. I couldn't wait until the sun came up the next morning so I could call my doctor. I made an appointment for later that day. My doctor confirmed she felt a mass and sent me for a mammogram. The mammogram confirmed there was a lump. "Two o'clock" was the location they kept using. The step that then followed was a breast ultrasound. A small machine glides over the "affected area" and shows the sonographer if the mass is something that can be drained like a cyst or if it is a solid mass. My ultrasound determined it was a solid mass. Next step. Biopsy. This procedure was so painful. They brought you into a dark room where you had to lie perfectly still so that they could extract tissue from the mass. I knew I was strong. I was a young mom, I worked since I was 15, and I had overcome so many things in life. Why did I feel so weak? All I wanted was someone to hold me and tell me it was nothing, but not for my story. Instead, I was alone in that cold dark room having a larger than life needle inserted by a stranger into my breast as I held my breath. I got up from the examining table more scared than when I laid down. I went home that Monday afternoon in pain. Physical pain from the

Holly Cotton

biopsy and emotional pain from the terror that awaited me. Then on Friday October 12th came, "the call"...

My nursing school curriculum consisted of clinical rotations on Fridays. You were assigned to a unit to shadow the nursing staff and help out as needed. Here comes the "slow motion" part. I remember every single detail. I was on a pediatric unit when my cell phone vibrated in my pocket. I saw the familiar number of the doctor's office. I ran into the restroom to answer the call. I managed to get out a shaky "Hello?" "Hello Holly, this is Dr. S. your biopsy results came back. It's cancer. It's very, very bad. You need to go see a surgeon. Call one of those doctors I gave you a business card for the other day." Not the notification I was anticipating. That was it, no I'm sorry, no empathy whatsoever in her voice. Definitely not the movie version where they call you into the office, have you sit in a big comfy chair, sit across from you and hand you tissues as you cry. Nothing. I was left standing there staring at my phone in the bathroom of the hospital with a blank face of disbelief.

I immediately knew I had to leave the unit I was on, there was no way I could continue the school rotation. I text my professor I needed to leave. I held my composure. I'm pretty proud of myself on this one. I remember gathering my belongings, smiling and thanking the staff for being so helpful and allowing me to observe them. Still no tears. Just shock. "Keep it together Holly" I kept telling myself in the elevator. As soon as I made it to the ground floor of the hospital and the doors opened, I saw my professor's face. She was standing there with worry in her eyes. I had been such a good student she knew something was wrong. Seeing the familiar face I burst out into tears. She held me. We walked over to a bench where she comforted me. She was a nurse practitioner as well as an instructor, so she was able to give me her medical insight on my cancer diagnosis. I don't know what we talked about for that hour, but I do remember these words as if she is telling me right now..."you are getting across that stage in May for graduation, if I have to push you in a hospital bed or wheel chair, you are going to cross that stage to graduate". It is in these situations that the most unexpected people make the biggest impact on your story. I will always remember my instructor's face and words. I will always be grateful that she gave me that motivation.

The forty minute commute home was the longest ride I ever drove. I thought of how I would need to tell my kids "your mom has breast cancer". They were my babies, only twelve and seven years old at the time. I

Holly Cotton

drove like a zombie, oblivious to the songs playing on the radio. Unaware of anything else except what my journey would be. Making turns by memory. Unable to focus on anything except the call. What would my treatment options be? Would I be sick? Who would take care of my kids? I practiced the words in my head of how I would break it to them. Gently in a long speech or just blurt it out? Should I offer the diagnosis with ice cream and a trip to the toy store? How would I tell my parents? They would be so worried about me. What if I died? Who would take care of everything? Do I want to be buried or cremated? The list just kept going. The thing I realized the most during my journey with breast cancer was that being sick is mostly about others. Telling them not to worry when you're scared to death. Trying to convince them that you won't die when you think you're dying. Trying to make them feel better about taking care of you if and when you can't take care of yourself. Looking back I wish I was selfish for once in my life. Allowing myself to worry about my own fears.

STRONG.

Chapter Two: So what's next?

When I got home it was 1:00pm. I knew my children would be home at 3:30. I cried for two hours. I mean really cried. Not tears for exes or frivolous things, but sobs of fear and pain that I could leave my children without a mother. I don't remember anything else about that afternoon. I tried over and over to think of what I was wearing, what my kids ate for dinner. It is just a big blur to me now. I remember them coming home from school and seeing me disheveled. They immediately looked like they were going to cry from my demeanor. I sat them down on the sofa and explained that I had some tests done and it showed that I had tested positive for breast cancer. I assured them that I was going to be okay a hundred times. My daughter cried. Cancer has such a definitive outcome. You die. So telling them was very difficult to do. My son asked some questions that I didn't have answers for. I reassured him we would figure it out together. We hugged and I held each child in an arm. Hundreds of kisses were imploded onto their foreheads and cheeks. We finished the evening watching a movie and embracing the time that we had.

The week that followed was very busy. I didn't have time to be sad. I didn't have time to feel sorry for myself. I just knew I needed to get this cancer out of me as soon as possible. I was in business mode. I knew what needed to happen. Monday morning I called one of the surgeons I had a business card for from my doctor's office. I was able to get a consultation appointment the next day. I was so relieved I chose the card that I did. This doctor was the best thing that could have happened to me. Being a nurse all I do is take care of other people. I needed someone to take care of me. She spoke to me like I was special. I remember her going over every detail. "Stage one, two o'clock, in situ". She drew pictures about cancer stages, the size of my tumor. She drew a little breast and showed me the lymph nodes that could be affected. I needed a tangible version to understand what I had ahead of me. She didn't miss a detail. She was patient, answered all my questions. I finally felt like I was being taken care of. I could lower my wall and let someone help me get through this hard time. Two options were given to me, a lumpectomy where they went in and took out the tumor or a mastectomy where they remove the entire breast. I was told because of my age, 36, there was a high percentage that I could be diagnosed with breast cancer again in my life. Therefore, the mastectomy option may be the best choice. I looked down and my little deflated breasts, I said I have no loyalty to these suckas! Take them off! So we decided, bilateral (both breasts) mastectomy. The process was "simple" she said. I believe when people say something is simple, they are trying to convince the other person not to worry about something they should actually be worried about. Anyway, she told me the process would be...wait for it...to cut my breasts under the nipple where the breast crease was. Then she would excise all the breast tissue I had under the skin. So basically skin my breast to the muscle. Obviously removing the lump, but also all the tissue from the side of my breasts close to my armpits to the breast tissue in the middle of my chest. Well isn't this more and more fun? We discussed nipples. She explained that usually they removed the nipple in mastectomies, as this includes breast tissue and could have cancer cells growing in them she said that we may be able to save my nipples based on the location of the lump, but that there would always be the risk that I could get breast cancer again in my nipples. With all the changes I said that it was a chance I was willing to take if possible. So our goal for surgery would be to "save the nips"! We discussed surgery dates, I said as soon as possible. I knew I had to stay focused on school so we arranged a surgery close to the Thanksgiving break, November 19, 2012. She referred me to a plastic surgeon for the reconstruction process. So much information. My mind was spinning. I was getting breasts taken off and new breasts put back on! How am I going to do this? How will I be able to take care of my kids, work, go to school?

So as directed I now scheduled an appointment with a plastic surgeon that specialized in breast reconstruction. I walked into his office and sat down waiting for my name to be called. I had no idea what this process even entailed. What exactly was reconstruction? There were numerous photo albums on the side and coffee tables. I opened one of the books and flipped through the pages. Nothing but boobs! Breasts that had been reconstructed were surprising to me. Some had nipples, some had a big scar where the nipples were, some were big some were flat, some had nipple tattoos. My stomach ached. How would I look? How would I wake up from surgery looking and feeling? I was not ready to deal with all of this! Strong Holly. Be strong Holly. It will work out Holly. I kept telling myself over and over. Finally my name was called. I sat on the office bed with the little robe thingy that barely covers you up waiting to see who this would be that was going to "reconstruct" me. Finally Dr. S walked in. He told me about the process. After the surgeon removed all of the breast tissue he would insert spacers. They are square little things that slowly expand the remaining breast tissue. They would already be inserted under my pectoral muscles when I woke up from surgery. Well this keeps getting better and better. Through everything we talked about and all the fear I felt, I just kept reminding myself I was getting this cancer lump removed and had a chance of holding my kids a little bit longer so I would do anything to stay alive.

During the week after the big diagnosis I knew I needed to tell my family and friends. I have a close group of friends from college, a sister and a few nieces I am close to. My father lived in Boston and my mother was still living in my hometown of Louisiana. I told my dad first. I remember dialing his number. Confused on how to say the words to him, I just blurted it out. I could tell he was in disbelief. Who thinks their healthy daughter has cancer? I told him my surgery date and he said he would be there to help me with the kids and recovery. Then I called my mom. She started crying as soon as I told her I had cancer. I spent the rest of the conversation comforting her and promised I wouldn't die. Next my girlfriends. At this point I was so tired of telling the whole diagnosis story. You're happy that you have people who care about you and want to know about your life, but its draining. Each time you tell the story you relive it. Sometimes you just want to forget what is going on. I made all four friends get on a conference call so I only had to tell my story one time. They did really well. No outbursts, no crying, not too many questions. The usual "we are praying for you", "you're going to be okay", was how they replied. I later learned that they had several conversations afterwards that involved crying. I was so relieved that they waited to cry after my call. I couldn't take having to comfort anyone else about my diagnosis. I called my sister. She had dealt with breast cancer first hand with her stepdaughter. Unfortunately, she died from her illness. Now here I was

STRONG.

telling her I had the same thing. I knew she was sacred. She was supportive and gave the usual condolences. The worst thing you can do when someone is going through something is to bring up someone else who had the same issue, or give an example of how someone got over a similar problem as you. You want that call to be about you. You want the conversation to be about you at that point. She made it completely about me. She knew she needed to be strong for me. I am very close to one of my nieces. She is actually only a year older than me and I grew up thinking she was my sister. Long story for the next book. I called her and she was actually my "cry to" person. She still is. She is brutally honest yet supportive. Exactly the type of comforting a strong person needs. We talked every day. She would let me cry to her on the phone. I did that with pretty much everyone I talked to during that time too, but more often with her. Although everyone was scattered around in other states, I felt the support and love from everyone. Times like this I realized, it is okay to need people. It is okay to lean on someone. Sometimes you just need someone else to tell you that you're not going to die. I didn't want my fear to be seen by my kids. I had to be strong for them. I never let them hear me on the phone crying or see me worried. I needed them to believe in me being okay as much as they believed in Santa Claus!

During the next month, as I was awaiting surgery, I spent a lot of time reading and researching. I bounced from website to website. Desperate to find the success stories. Hoping to find some motivation to stay strong. I started reading blogs about cancer survivors who hadn't survived. People all going through the same thing I was. Note to my future self, never do that again. You get so scared and obsessed by everyone else's version. Worried about if and when you would have the same outcome. Everyone has their own story to tell and write. Their own road to walk. The last thing I want to do is give unsolicited advice. You can read that same line on a hundred greeting cards. I can assure you, when you are going through something; the last thing you want to hear is some hoity toity line about writing your own story. All you want is to survive what is going on, not caring about it being something that will make you a stronger person. Everyone wants to help. It is hard for your loved ones to see you going through this pain. To feel so helpless. When tragedy strikes you see how little control you actually have in this world. Everyone wants to be that support person for you that makes everything alright again. I recall getting so many pink shirts and ink pens from friends and family members that I had breast cancer paraphernalia coming out of my ears. I still wear some of the survivor shirts with pride that I received. I spent my evenings reading the countless books that were given to me written by cancer victims. I appreciated each and every little gesture. I remember my job throwing me an awesome pink party. They had all of my favorite foods and desserts. The way to my happiness is always food related. Honestly, that was something I really needed. They treated me like I was still normal. We laughed and listened to music. I wasn't surrounded by the sad faces of people looking at me as if I were dying. I often think about what would have really helped in this timeline. Reality: I think it is dependent on the person. For myself, I wish I had someone to drop off meals or help my kids with their homework. The simple day to day things that keep your household running. I remember rolling into this little ball of depression that I didn't feel up to doing anything. Then I would be more depressed because of the guilt that I wasn't. That I wasn't being the best mom. That I didn't want to fix gourmet meals even in my last days before surgery. So for me, having a person helping with those day to day activities would have been the most useful instead of sending me another pink pen. Just something to think about when you want to support someone. Most of the time it is not going to be the

Holly Cotton

grand gesture that they need, it's the overlooked smaller things that make the biggest difference.

Chapter Three:

Goodbye Breasts

Finally the morning of surgery came. I woke up at 5am. I went into each of my kids' rooms. I kissed them and held them one last time while I still had the strength to hold them. I told them I was going to be okay. My dad had made it to Houston and would be home with the kids after I got out of surgery. I talked to him about my wishes if I didn't wake up. My husband drove me to the hospital that morning. We drove in silence. I remember him trying to be funny to lighten the mood. It didn't work. I was scared to death. I couldn't even think straight. I was nauseous. I felt like I was going to pass out. We got to the hospital and I checked in. The usual check in process ensued. After vital signs, paperwork and blood samples they put you in the pre-op waiting area until it's time to roll you to the operating room. I remember lying there looking across at the other small rooms. Wondering what they were getting operated on. What their stories were. My boss at the time showed up. She sat next to my bed for a while. We talked and joked about the workplace. She was a great person to have in my life at that time. Again, that unexpected person that makes the biggest impact. My surgeon came in to say hello. She drew lines on my chest to set up her perimeter for surgery. I remember laughing with her and reminding her that the goal was to "save the nips". She said she would do everything possible for the campaign. Then this happened, something I didn't know I needed so badly until it happened. She held my hand and asked if she could pray with me. Caught off guard I said "of course". She prayed for God to guide her hands to ensure I was safe. She prayed for my kids to be safe. She prayed for me to come out of surgery healed. It was a very holistic approach and I definitely appreciated her reminding me that there is always a higher power that controls our fate. Then she left. My plastic surgeon came next. More drawing and measuring. He was a very serious person, so I enjoyed being funny and making him smile. We had a great pow wow and then he left to prepare. Only one of my girlfriends was able to make it to the hospital that day. She came to the back and sat with me until the rolled me back. I remember the anesthesiologist giving me the white liquid through my IV and watching the lights on the ceiling passing as they rolled me down the hallway. My last memory was me crying, was this it? What if I died? What would I look like when I woke up? And then a big light as the operating doors opened.

I woke up to the voice of a nurse saying "take a deep breath Holly". I was alive! I didn't even care about breasts or scars. I was alive. I sat in recovery for a while. I remember I was so happy to be alive I couldn't stop talking. I talked to my nurse about frivolous things. I talked to a male nurse across the room about his socks. I remember they were colorful. I didn't want to stop talking because I thought maybe I was dreaming. Finally they rolled me to my hospital room. My kids were there. I can't find the words to describe how happy I was to see them. My dad was in the room waiting for me to come in also. They tell me I was very loopy at the time. My dad said I asked him to bring me a ham. That means

Holly Cotton

I was feeling much better. That first night was intense. I couldn't lift my arms up. I had to get up to go to the bathroom. Connected to wires and plugs and cords. It was a long night of pain. I felt like there was an elephant on my chest. So much pressure. I was all wrapped up with bandages. I just wanted to sleep. The story that followed from my friends was that they all sat in the waiting room during my surgery. It took four hours for the doctors to cut off my breasts and insert the spacers. They had all camped out in the waiting room. My boss and her husband, my best friend, my kids, husband, and my dad. They waited patiently for me to get out of the operating room. I was so appreciative. When people do things like that you realize how much they love you. When you feel all alone it's nice to reflect on stories like this and realize that you aren't.

The next morning my doctors came in to check on me and I asked to go home. They checked the bandages. This would be the first time I looked at my chest without breasts. I slowly looked down at the bandages. My surgeon lifted the elastic bandage on my right breast. I saw a nipple. They saved the nips! My doctor explained that there was still a chance that my nipples could become necrotic. This meant that because of the trauma of surgery and so many blood vessels and nerves being removed with the tissue that the nipples may not receive a good blood supply and die. Turning black and falling off or requiring additional surgery. Well isn't that just delightful? The fun never stops! I was actually surprised that my chest looked almost the same way it did before surgery. There were two large square bumps where the spacers were. I couldn't see anything else because of the bandages. They showed me how to empty the drains I had connected to each side of my chest collecting fluid. They let me go home that morning before lunch. The ride home was the worst. I read somewhere to pack a pillow for the ride home so you can brace your breasts for the trip. I held the pillow close to my chest and squeezed hard as the car backed up. Trying to stop the bumps in the road from making my chest move. Every brake and turn felt like someone was hitting me in the chest. I would hate to know how things would have gone if I didn't have the pillow. When I got home I went straight to bed. I think I slept for the rest of the day. I woke up and took another dose of pain medication. As I got up to go to the restroom I caught a glimpse of myself as I waddled by the mirror. I felt like I was looking at a monster. What happened to me? Why did this happen to me? I began to cry. When you feel like you had everything figured out and it is all taken away it is very depressing. I went from being, what I thought was, the healthiest to not even being able to

Holly Cotton

stand up straight. The stress of getting the lump removed was over, now what? I couldn't even lift my arms up. How can I find the positive side of this? I referred to myself as a T-Rex for the rest of my recovery. It's a very accurate analogy if you are trying to picture how a person looks when all of their breast tissue is removed. You have to keep your arms right by your sides to prevent the muscles from moving and causing a shooting pain that goes down to your feet. Trying to balance being sad and in pain with being alive and still fighting was a hard feat. I went back and forth with the guilt of being alive as so many people had died from cancer. Here I was crying over some incisions and others had succumbed to its devastation. Why was I so selfish? I never thought for once I would be one of those "breast cancer people" with the pink ribbons and shirts. This is where reality set in. I was so focused on the surgery to get the lump removed. To survive surgery. Now that was over. All I was left with was finding the strength to recover.

Chapter Four: The Recovery

The first morning after surgery I thought a bus passed through my room and ran over me. Then backed up and ran over me again. I had never felt a pain like this before. Just to move was an excruciating. I tried to stay still like a statue. I hated when I had to go to the bathroom because I was forced to move. I slept sitting up. I had a pillow under each arm for support. I took a pain pill every four hours. I cried that I was hurting. I cried that this happened to me. I cried that I couldn't hold my phone. I cried that my back hurt. All I wanted was to lie on my stomach. An impossible feat at this time. I slept the first few days. Didn't eat much of anything. I would get up to empty my drains and then just go back into bed and go to sleep. Finally I decided I needed to look at my newfound scars in the face and see what my road to recovery really looked like. I opened the ace bandage wrapped around my torso. I looked at my body in the mirror. I saw an incision that followed the crease under my breasts that went from right under my armpit to the middle of my chest. I saw the dressings that covered it. A little reddish brown line where the blood had collected. I still felt like I had been filleted like a fish. Wow. They were really gone. I really had surgery. I would really have these large scars on my body for the rest of my life. I felt myself going down a road of depression. I was so angry at myself. Why was I being like this? Why couldn't I be strong? Why couldn't I pick myself up? After a few days I said, "this is it Holly". No more pity party. I got up from the bed and started sitting on the sofa. I started eating with my family. I started brushing my teeth by myself. I was able to start showering. Every day I became more and more strong. I refused to be beat. I was going to get back to where I was.

The hardest part of my surgery was that it was the week before Thanksgiving. I went into the operating room Friday morning and Thanksgiving would fall on the following Thursday. For the last twelve years I had prepared a feast for my little family. My son would come into the kitchen and peel sweet potatoes, base the turkey. From the time he could stand he helped me fix dinner. Now here I was, unable to even pick up a knife, much less prepare a feast. My daughter was so excited to prepare dishes like her Barbie did in the doll dream house kitchen. Her little hands could barely hold the utensils she was using. She had the most adorable little apron with her name monogramed onto the front. I felt so guilty that I was ruining their holiday. How would this affect their memories of Thanksgiving? Were they disappointed because I couldn't do anything? While I was asleep in my room my friends brought their versions of Thanksgiving to help out on the holiday. I got out of the bed Thanksgiving Day for a bit. I saw that my dad bought a ham and attempted to cook side dishes. My kids had an input in his menu so they chose only the dishes they wanted, no unwanted vegetables. My father's girlfriend, who was also visiting to help out, is Italian. She prepared a special authentic Italian dish for our family. I realized with the help of everyone else that this Thanksgiving would be special instead of ruined. My kids would have a recollection of what Thanksgiving really means. The gathering of families. Everyone coming together and spending time together. My surgery would prove to be an undercover blessing. I just needed to get better to realize it.

A week after surgery I had to finally sit down and meet with an oncologist. I walked into his office and signed in. As I found a vacant seat I looked around the office. So many people in the waiting room looked like they were dying. I saw a woman with all pink on. Breast cancer obviously. A man with an oxygen tank was sitting across from me. He weighed about ninety pounds. I thought "is this what is going to happen to me now?" I never really thought about a plan for after surgery. I didn't know my options or what would come next. I sat there scared of what my fate might be. Finally my name was called to go into a patient room. The doctor came in and spoke to me about pathology results. After surgery they sent my tumor off to a lab and test the cancer cells that combined to form my tumor. He explained that I was triple positive. Meaning that my tumor was caused by hormones. If we stopped hormone production in my body, we could stop new cancer cells from forming or growing. He said my course of treatment would be Tamoxifen. A small pill I would take every day for ten years that inhibited estrogen production. I would not need chemotherapy or radiation. Whew! Those were the most beautiful words I ever heard. I was so worried about how I would finish school being sick from chemotherapy. How I would go back to work being so sick. He explained that the medication would put my body in a menopausal state when it started working. I thought about it and determined any state would be fine with me if I could be alive. I stopped by on my way home to pick up my new medication. I started it that day. That has pretty much been my entire philosophy since the first day I found out I had cancer. I don't care what it is or what it takes; as long as I'm alive I will do whatever I need to. It is a very humbling experience. The things you fretted over so much, hair, make up clothes. The material items you couldn't live without. All those things go out the window when you stare death in the face. When you are left to pick up the pieces and rebuild your life you hardly care if your eyelashes are long or your underwear matches your bra.

Finally, around two weeks post-op I started feeling a little better. My body still hurt like heck, but I was feeling better about life and the whole recovery process. My family and friends called or text every day to check on me. My kids were actually being good and doing their homework. There was not the usual yelling and fighting that consumed my house. The first day I was able to shave my legs was such an accomplishment. I actually cried tears of joy! Being able to stretch my arms far enough to reach my shins and shave upwards without excruciation pain. Now we're talking! I felt my independence slowly creeping back into me. Right after surgery the skin was so tight and painful around my chest that I had to stand at the sink in a hunched over position to brush my teeth. Gradually, I was able to start standing a little straighter. I could be in the bathroom without someone having to help me do every simple task. I still couldn't raise my hands to wash my hair. I was dying to put my hair in a ponytail. I had no clue how many muscles and how much strength it took to make a ponytail! I still had to sleep sitting up, propping my arms on pillows so they didn't hang down causing my chest muscles to stretch. I would think about all the things I could no longer do, how I had taken so much for granted. When I started walking around my house again I was so excited to wash a dish. However; the excitement has long passed. I still looked like a T-Rex, but I knew I was getting better. That's the great thing about pain. It doesn't last. It sucks to go through it, but then when you look back you remember how you overcame it. Not just the physical pain, but the fear and sadness that cause the emotional struggle.

The process for reconstruction is an odd one. Every week you go to your plastic surgeon's office. They insert a needle into your chest. The nurse slowly inserts saline, approximately 50-100mL into the spacers. This is to make the tissue gradually stretch out. I was told that the tissue was still much traumatized from the surgery and over pulling it or causing more trauma could cause it to die. This would mean that I needed to go back to the operating room to remove the dead tissue. So I thought "yes, this gradual weekly thing sounds like a much better option!" So every week I went in and watched the nurse use a magnet on my breast to find the port for the needle. Watched her insert this needle into my chest. Watched the expander grow slowly. My chest would always feel like an elephant was sitting on it after the procedure. It felt so tight I could hardly breathe. The good thing about a mastectomy is that they also remove nerves with the breast tissue. Pain indicators. So although you are watching the process you can't feel anything! Finally, a positive thing to all this! After a day or two the pressure subsided and I could breathe again. Four weeks later I determined that my breasts were large enough. I had always had small breasts from being so active. Why start now having large breasts? So we decided on a "C" cup size and scheduled surgery for the next week to remove the expanders and insert a silicone implant.

The second surgery wasn't hard. I knew what to expect. I knew how I would feel to go into the operating room. My doctor came into the preoperative waiting room and

Holly Cotton

did his usual bout of drawing lines and dots. I was rolled into the operating room and again, the big light as the doors opened then nothing. I woke up in the recovery room with no memory of surgery. The nurse gave me all these discharge instructions. She said something about wearing the compression bra for a certain amount of time, lifting, pulling and other things you should not be telling someone who just woke up from surgery because they don't retain any information you've given them. I made it home and back to resting. I actually felt so much lighter now that the large box shaped spacers were gone. I slept the first night like I always did, sitting up with the pillows. The pain was not like the first surgery. I didn't need the pain medication as often as my mastectomy. I was able to fall asleep that night without any tossing and turning. This time it was different, there wasn't the fear of cancer. There wasn't the fear of the unknown. I had been through the worse, so this time I was prepared. The next day I woke up and looked down at my special bra. Hopefully one day some inventor will make these a tad bit more stylish. Just stretchy material and tons of clasps. Overall my chest seemed normal looking. I just looked like I would if I had a breast augmentation. As I stood up I figured I needed to see what I really looked like. I walked into the bathroom and looked at myself in the floor length mirror. No drains this time. No gauze and ace wraps making me look like a mummy. I opened the clasps in the front of the bra...the incisions were right over my previous incisions, so no new scars. I actually looked a little bit normal. I was feeling like I may not always be a monster. I might actually be able to live with these shiny new perky breasts.

Holly Cotton

Chapter Five:

What's your purpose?

In the weeks and months that followed I fell back into my old routine. I was still in my nursing program. I was still working fulltime. Not as many hours, but still working. I reflected on what I had been through, but not only myself. The things that so many others were going through. I started looking at my life. All of the things I had taken for granted. Before cancer I would talk to my sister once a month, tops. Throughout

Holly Cotton

my journey we talked every day. I felt closer to her than I ever had. Other people in my family, same thing. I had gone years without speaking to cousins. Not out of anger, just because of life. Now I was meeting my third and fourth cousins, extended family members. I would wake up happy to be alive and hop out of bed instead of slumping into a pile of bones onto the floor. I realized when I could lose everything that I needed to focus on things that actually mattered. To appreciate the things I had taken for granted for so long. I knew that I was still here for a purpose. I just needed to find out what that purpose was.

I eventually graduated in May as my professor had told me I would. My family and friends were so proud of me. I was proud of me. While other students were stressing over the next test, I was showing up to class with drains tucked into the waist band of my scrub pants. As they met in the library to study, I was on my way to work full time. Not saying my journey was harder than anyone else's, but it sure wasn't easy. When I walked across that stage to get my degree my eyes were swollen from the tears of happiness. I looked into the audience and saw my kids standing and cheering for me. They were just as much a part of this accomplishment as me. My son had helped me many nights with dinner and household chores so I could study. My daughter helped me adjust my laptop using my two arm prop pillows because I couldn't lift my arms up. We had all done it; I was just the one walking across the stage. After graduation I decided to switch to a different job. I took a new job as a director of a facility. I was trying to get back to working out, but I was still sore from the nerve regeneration and I couldn't do anything that involved using chest or arm muscles. Through all of this I was still searching for my purpose. How could I give back? How could I help someone else? What could I do so the rest of my life meant something? I knew I needed a job, but I also knew I needed to give back. Someone sent me a picture one day that said "I did not survive cancer to die from stress". I thought, wow, this is reality. I didn't go through all that pain to come out on the other side letting negativity kill me. I quit my job. I needed to do something where I was making an impact. Where my work was not surrounded by stress and misery. I decided to start teaching nursing students at a community college. I will be eternally grateful for my instructor that helped me through my journey with cancer. I wanted to be that person for someone else. Whether it is just a simple life decision or a major event like I went through, I finally felt that I found a career where I could give back.

Holly Cotton

I remember celebrating my one year cancer free status. I posted on Facebook that I had survived the year. I had accomplished my goals. I had found a job I enjoyed doing. But what else did I have? I spent the day reflecting on my purpose. I remember my brain shifting from the "why me?" as in feeling sorry for myself to a "why me?" as in what was the cosmic purpose for putting me through all of this and allowing me to survive. For allowing me to come out stronger than I was before. As I said before, being sick is a humbling experience. I thought my life was all figured out. I didn't need anyone. I could do everything alone. Then you get something that happens to you where you can't even wipe your own bottom and realize you actually do need people. And not only that you need them, but that it's okay to let them be there for you. For once in my life I finally accepted that I needed help with taking care of my kids. I accepted that I couldn't do everything by myself. It is okay to ask for help, to let people be there for you. Accepting help inadvertently makes you stronger.

My sister is 15 years older than me. She was a teenage mom. She and I had an odd relationship. I was like one of her kids as we were all around the same ages. She even spanked me. I am still bitter about this; we will discuss it in the next book. After my diagnosis, we began talking almost every day. She listened to me cry and whine for six months straight. Always with positive reinforcement to make me feel better. We discussed my pain, the scars, and my fears about treatment, and fear about getting cancer again. Not one time was she not there for my call. We often discuss how getting sick is the last thing you want a loved one to go through, but in this instance I got my sister back. I got my family back. I thought I was fine with just my kids, but was the purpose of me getting sick to show me I wasn't? I wasn't the Wonder Woman I wore on my t-shirts. I was actually a scared and timid person during my sick stage. Same with my girlfriends. We would go months without talking and then during my sick stage, talked to them almost every day. We were just as close as when we were in college again. When we lived in each other's dorm rooms. We couldn't even eat without checking in with each other. Then life comes along and takes you on your separate paths. We were all reconnected.

Again, what was my purpose? Then it hit me. Could my purpose be to help other people? I had been a nurse all of my life. Helping people during their sicknesses. I had always taken care of other's physical ailments, but what about the emotional side of sickness? Now I realize how hard it is. We expect the person to be okay in a few days following surgery. When the incisions heal and the scars start to fade. But that isn't all that needs to heal. I am still emotionally scarred from the insensitive phone call my doctor gave me to inform me I had cancer. I am still emotionally sick from the fear that I have cancer again. Where is it? Do I have a brain tumor? Are there some cancer cells having a party in my big toe? I realized that tons of people are feeling the same way as me. My purpose was to let them know that it is okay to feel this way. It is okay to be angry and scared. It is okay to take time to heal your mind not just your body. We rush into life. No pain must mean that I have to start living life again. My purpose would be to find these people that needed to know how strong they were and make them know we are not alone in this world. My purpose would not only reach people who were cancer patients or survivors, but all people. It was at this point the development of "Strong Squad" began to formulate. Everyone has something in life they have gone through that challenges them. We sit around feeling like there is no way will overcome this issue. It may be a death, a bad relationship, a terrible job, and things with children or family members. Your obstacle is not better or worse than mine. We are all in need of finding the strength that lies within us.

After my one year Cancerversary, I knew it was time to fulfill my purpose and make each day count. My scars had faded from the big incisions they once were. I could see the faint white line when I looked at myself. My original reaction of disgust turned into one of proudness! Instead of the "look at those scars" as ugly, I said "LOOK AT THOSE SCARS!" They were beautiful to me.   A constant reminder of what I had gone through...AND SURVIVIED! I was a completely different person than I was the year before. Now that my pain had subsided I started working out again. Although I must say those first few months were tormenting. I would cry I was in so much pain. I went from one arm push-ups before cancer to barely holding myself up off the floor. Every day I pushed and got stronger. I vowed that I would never be this weak again! I started posting pictures on social media and getting feedback from men and women. "Wow Holly, I can't believe you are back to working out". "You are so inspirational". Me? Inspirational? Not a word I ever thought would describe me. Then again, my "purpose". I was showing people if I could get back into working out after all I went through, maybe them starting was doable. Maybe they would want to join me in getting healthy.

What about my purpose as a mom? During the cancer process I cried so many times about the possibility of not being able to hold my children or touch them again. I couldn't let myself get complacent and take it for granted now that I was doing better. I refused to let life get in the way of cherishing the moments I had left with them. Could I possibly in some way pass on how to be strong to my kids? What changes did I need to make to show them I was different, that our relationship was different? I knew I needed to get my priorities straight, focus on my purpose. Focus on being a mom again, not just someone who takes care of kids and bills. I was not going to waste the second half of my life. I never let my kids walk out the door without telling them I love them. Even as teenagers I make sure I kiss them goodnight. Life is so uncertain. How long do I have left? How long do they have left? I know that when I'm looking death in the eyes again I will know I am leaving my children with the best memories I could. I loved them with all that I knew how to. My story is not about saying my parenting is better than anyone else's. We all love our babies. I am just reminding you to show that love. You can have all the thoughts in your head, but make sure they know it. Don't hold all the goodness inside. Let it out like a giant firework. Let the love sparks consume those you love because one day you won't be able to. That's the part you think about. You will never regret the effort; you will regret that you held back. This isn't just related to children. Love your dog, your husband or wife, your step kids, extended family. I'm trying to make you refocus on

STRONG.

STRONG.

those roles and remember your purpose in someone else's life. Don't waste valuable time.

Holly Cotton

Chapter Six:

Awakening the Strong

After I started exercising, I decided to run in one of those mud races. What was I thinking? Oh yes I remember, to show my daughter that being a woman means being strong. Showing my son that women are more than pretty faces and breasts. It was the first time I attempted one of these races. I remember it being chilly as I tried to re-evaluate again why I would possibly

Holly Cotton

want to get wet. I was worried an implant would pop out as I climbed over ropes and walls. How would my body react? It was a long 3.1 miles. That's what the sign said the race was, but I think they added another two miles to the race track. When I climbed over the last wall I remember looking over to my left. I saw a little pink hoodie on top of a person. I remembered it was my daughter's jacket. From the top of the wall I saw her standing there on the sideline with her little fist up yelling "go mom!" My son actually captured her on film and I still cherish this picture. It reminded me that no matter how many times you fall, no matter how you do things in life. Those that love you will be right there on the sideline cheering for whatever crazy and over the top thing you are trying to accomplish! That was all the motivation I needed to use every ounce of my strength to climb over the back side of the wall back to the ground and spring over that finish line. That's life for you though; motivation comes from the most unexpected events. Synopsis of the story is I completed the 5K obstacle mud dash. Since that first race I have completed fifteen to twenty other races. My family even started running the obstacle races with me. It's wonderful how strength can be contagious. My purpose...

STRONG.

The hardest thing I've had to be strong for since cancer was my mother dying. We always had an awkward relationship. I know she loved me and my two sisters dearly. The problem was she always kept a wall up from showing us that she loved us. I would tell her I loved her when I visited her and she would never say it back. My whole life I yearned to have a close relationship with my mother. I wanted her to be proud of me. I will never know how she felt about me. After cancer we did develop a sense of closeness. I refused to let either one of us die without saying we loved each other. So I tried to visit often, thinking she would always be here. Her health began to decline last year. Her medical diagnosis was "failure to thrive". She became bed constrained because of leg contractures. She developed a wound on her tail bone. We eventually had to put her in a facility. My sister and I felt sick that we had to do such a thing. She was so stubborn; she refused to come to Texas to stay with me. She refused to stay with my sisters. So we had no other options. I often wonder when did she lose her sense of purpose? When did she decide death was better than life? She was put on hospice. She was barely eating or drinking. I knew I had to go visit her in Louisiana before she passed away and I was filled with regret. I booked a plane ticket and flew in on Wednesday evening. When I saw how frail she looked in that bed I began to sob. My mother was the strongest woman I knew. She was mean; she would crack a stranger in the head with her cane without blinking. She would crack us in the head with her cane without blinking. Now here she was lying in the bed dying. I visited all day and night when I was in town. As a nurse I've seen death so many times. I have been on the other side so many times. Comforting families, offering comfort to the patient. Now here the roles were reversed yet again. I knew I needed to be strong for her. I accepted that this was her peace. I remember lying in the hospital bed with her. My head on her chest. She whispered "I am so miserable". She was in so much pain. My choices were to be selfish and beg her to fight through the pain, or give her comfort in letting go. I chose the latter. I told her that she had done a great job being a mother. She had given us the tools to be strong independent women like she was. That she had raised us the best she could and that it was okay to let us go. I spent the weekend with her and knew in my soul it would be the last weekend I saw her. I had to get back to Texas and work, life. Monday morning at 5am I walked into her room. She wasn't speaking at that point. She was lying in bed. I could sense the smell of death; I knew her body was shutting down. I lay across her chest and followed her breaths. Up and down my head went with her life slowly exiting her. She was no longer responsive. As I lay on her chest I told her again that I loved her, I told her again that it was ok to leave us. I told her we knew she was hurting and if it was her time to go we would all be okay. As I looked into her face I saw a tear roll down her cheek. I had always taught my students that hearing was the last sense to leave the body. Now here in my own journey I witnessed it firsthand. I knew she heard me. I knew she loved me. I knew she was proud of me. I knew I couldn't be selfish and ask her to stay for me. Strong. Strong comes in so many versions. She was strong for accepting her fate. We were strong for letting her go. I knew I would never see my mother again as I left that room. I could barely walk up the hallway. How do you willingly walk away knowing you will never see that person again. I got on my plane at 8 am to head back to Texas. I received the phone call right after lunch that she was gone. Just like that.

I have tons of stories to share about being strong. Like the time I fought off an attempted mugger in the parking lot with a compact umbrella. I stopped at the store to get toilet paper one morning. I was walking back to my car from the store when I felt my arm feel like it was being pulled out of its socket. Not one to back down, I DID survive cancer. I used the umbrella I had wrapped around my other wrist to hit the attacker in the head multiple times. Causing him to start crying and running away. Yes, I know, not the smartest thing to do, but my instincts took over. Thank goodness it was a rainy day or else I may not have had that umbrella! Then there was the time I swam with dolphins in Cabo. I am deathly ill of bodies of water that have "things" swimming around. I absolutely love the beach, but I am more a frolicker. So when I waddled into that pen with dolphins, I thought "wow, I have really grown in my quest for strength". Of course all I could really think was "please don't touch me Mr. Dolphin" during the experience. I overcame that fear. Strength is just that. No matter what the circumstance is, it is about looking it in the eyes and conquering whatever it is. I ended the dolphin excursion with a very cute pic of me actually kissing the dolphin. Then there was the time I got an award for being one of the top 150 nurses in Houston. Strength in my career. The fact that I was chosen out of thousands of nurses. Little old me. I attended the luncheon with the other nurses, proud of how much I had accomplished in my nursing career. Graduating after my cancer diagnosis I decided to continue my education. I chose an online school this time. I finished my master's degree in four months. All stories of strength. Another instance let me add "afraid of heights" to my long list of fears. When I got to the top floor of the Sears Tower in Chicago I thought there was no way I was stepping into that little glass box a million stories above ground. Remember strong. I walked out onto that ledge and even glanced down. Yes, it was a millisecond, but I still did it. These things are simple. They are funny. Being strong isn't always about being serious. It is about taking the lemons in life and making the best lemonade possible. It is about using those fears as motivators to come outside of the little boxes we put ourselves in. The limits we put on ourselves. We can have fun, but not too much fun. We can be strong, but not too strong. Strong is mental strength. Strong is dedication to completing a goal. Strong is leaving something painful to find something better. Strong is stepping out of your comfort zone. It is not always about giant events. Those are the things we remember most, but the day to day achievements are what truly help us define our strong. What about the loved ones that are going through your rough time with you? The people left to deal with the loss if something happens to you. They must find their strong too. Our friends watching us deal with a bad situation and offering as much support as they can. Knowing they cannot change the circumstances for you. Watching someone fight requires strength just as the person fighting does.

Holly Cotton

Unable to take away the pain, feeling helpless. All of these things define strength as well.

My story is no more important than yours. We all come out stronger after something challenging. That's not what this book is about. This book is not about my life. It is about how to use my experiences to help you find your strength. To define your strong so that you can live the best life you can. You only get one shot at this. Make sure you are making the most out of it.

Holly Cotton

Chapter Seven: Not again!

So now here I am, alive. Five years after my initial diagnosis. I go to my oncologist every six months. I am still on that pill for another four years. What happens after that tenth year? I don't know. I'll write another book to tell you when I find out.

Last year I went to my well women's visit. I had switched to a new physician right after "the call". I am still emotionally scarred from my first doctor's tone and

Holly Cotton

attitude about my diagnosis. She never saw me after that call. Never followed up with me to ensure I had surgery, that I was I alive. Nothing. Being a nurse I know it is easy to desensitize traumatic events, but this was my event and I was bitter about it. After that, I refused to associate with anyone except empathetic professionals. People who cared about me and my health. So I switched to a lovely lady doctor. She would laugh at all my jokes. Big plus for me. That appointment she felt something "concerning" on my abdomen. "You gotta be kidding me" I thought. Here we go again. My oncologist had talked to me numerous times about my risks of getting uterine, ovarian, or cervical cancer related to my breast cancer diagnosis. So back to the ultrasound room. The room was so quiet. The sonographer kept clicking and measuring. My stomach was in my throat. What was she seeing? Of course she can't tell you what her opinion is. She would click and scrutinize the screen, then smile at me as to reassure me there was nothing there. Finally she was done, back to the patient room. My doctor looked at the black and white blurs on the computer screen and her reply was "there is something complex and concerning on your right ovary". And this means what exactly? I thought I was out of the danger zone. I'm back to normal, living my life again. After a lengthy discussion we decided on a total hysterectomy with removing everything except my other ovary, unless he was acting crazy when they cut me open. We scheduled surgery for a few weeks later.

When I had my first diagnoses a mutual friend introduced me to a girl that I went to high school with but had never met. She had been diagnosed with breast cancer a year before me and had undergone chemotherapy and surgery. We connected and became close. We talked about different things that happen to your body during this recovery. We talked about our fears. We were "survivor sisters". At the time I had my sonography and was scheduling surgery, I learned she had been diagnosed with breast cancer again and it had spread all over her internal organs. A survivor's worse nightmare! I was devastated! She was so beautiful and strong. She looked healthy. She had just had a baby and now here she was with cancer again. I monitored her social media posts closely. They were praying for the chemotherapy to work. For the tumors to shrink. I would like to tell you she won round two, but she didn't. She died that month surrounded by her family. I was not only sick because of her death, but sick about what was going on with me! I was terrified of what they would find when they opened me up to remove my uterus and ovary. Thank goodness my support team was in place. I cried to all my family and friends this time. I didn't hold it in like the first time. I knew being strong was about allowing you to be weak at times, about leaning on others.

Counting the weeks down until my surgery was depressing me. I dreaded that I would once again be weak. I was terrified about having to deal with the pain. More scars. More uncertainty. Finally the day of my hysterectomy came. My son, who was now eighteen, drove me to the hospital. It was his birthday. I felt like the worst mom ever. He followed the gurney as they pushed me down the hallway to the operating room. Kissed my forehead at the intersection of the operating room and the waiting room and assured me I would be ok. He was so grown up. I remember the tears rolling down my cheeks before the light from the operating room shined upon me. Then I woke up in the recovery room, I was relieved. I had survived yet another surgery. This time there was pain. Indescribable pain. I couldn't get comfortable. I kept asking for pain medication. I held a pillow over my abdomen hoping it would dull the pain. It didn't. Here I was again, alive, but the unknown journey to getting better awaited me. Finally I was stable and wheeled by a nurse to my hospital room. As I was being transported I thought about the recovery that awaited me. When would I know if it was ovarian cancer they had removed? What else was taken out during my procedure? I felt sad that I had to be alone yet again. I thought of why hadn't I moved on by now in my love life? How I wished I had someone waiting for me that would hold my hand and take care of me. When the door of my hospital room opened the first thing I saw was my niece sitting in the rocking chair next to the bed. I didn't know she was coming from Louisiana to be with me, but there she was. Like the cutest lil old grandma in her rocker I ever saw in the world. I was so relieved. Being single has downfalls at times like this. When you want someone to hold you. However she was the best non-boyfriend I could have asked for. She took great care of me. I can't wait to return the favor. There is a closeness that comes from wiping someone's butt. A closeness of seeing someone's nether regions that can't be explained. A love that can never be repaid.

The next morning my doctor came in to see me. She showed me the surgical pictures of my ovaries and what she had removed. All of my female reproductive organs removed, a cervix, a uterus, two fallopian tubes and the "concerning" ovary were sent to pathology for testing. The outcome of that report would determine if I had cancer again and what my next steps in life would be. I went home and recovered. After five days I got a call from my doctor's office. This time it was so much different. The nurse was soft with her words. When I

Holly Cotton

heard "the pathology was negative for cancer cells" I felt like a thousand pounds were lifted off of my soul. I knew recovery from surgery would be difficult, but I was so relieved that I did not have to endure another bout of cancer. All the fears that go along with the treatment. I called my friends and family. I started the conversation with each of them saying I had bad news. Then I would say "sorry but you're still stuck with me! No cancer!" I thought it was hilarious, them not so much. I had hit another speed bump in life, but I was still moving. That's the great thing about living. You may pause in one area for a while, but you can always keep moving. It may not be in the direction you wanted. I surely did not want a hysterectomy, but I was still moving. I was still fulfilling my purpose.

Holly Cotton

Chapter Eight: No Regrets

There are a thousand quotes about seizing the day. Yet, how many of us are actually living up to this omen? I know I am. Looking at death makes you wake up. Since my diagnoses I have traveled around the world. Before cancer I would put off things for tomorrow. I would wait until summer time to go on a trip. I figured I would always be around to see my kids laughing and living their lives. Then when you're told that the opportunity could be taken away, you wake up. Now all those quotes make sense. My purpose. To show others how to stop and smell the roses. To stop making excuses. Life is a mixture of struggles and happy events. You only appreciate the happy events after a struggle. The goal is to find the perfect balance of more happy than struggle. To get out of that dark place to enjoy the good times awaiting you. A year after my first surgery my family decided to take a trip to Disney World for Christmas. I had been there before several times with my kids, but this would be the first time to go with my sister, nieces and the extended family members. It was the most miserable vacation I have ever been on. The people!! My toes got stomped on until I didn't think I had toenails left. Every time I wanted to knock someone out I would see my kids laughing and it calmed my soul. The look on my kids' faces when they saw all the Christmas lights and the action, priceless. I would go back for three more Christmases to see those smiles again. My family and I embraced our new closeness. We began to take family vacations several times a year. We would spend weeks going back and forth about the traveling details. We would get sick of talking to each other. Then right when we missed each other again it was time to go on our trip. New York City, Las Vegas, the Grand Canyon, Smoky Mountains, Bahamas...the list goes on and on. I recently took my kids to Italy. It was my first time being in Europe as well. Definitely a culture shock. The whole time they were grumpy and complained about mostly everything. "We are in Italy, of course they will always have pasta and pizza on the menu" was a daily statement at meal time. It was a long eight days. I remember telling them, "you're going to get some culture exposure that you can talk to your children about if it kills me!" They still chose to be cranky teenagers. You won't win every battle, especially the one making your kids appreciate something. I take pride that they are living a totally different life than we did growing up. Now I hear them talking to their friends of all the places they have visited. If I die today I can die in peace knowing that I seized every day I had with my family and friends. No regrets.

As I began to slow down and enjoy life, I started focusing on the small things. I wanted to savor every day events as if they were my last time trying them. Besides traveling, I realized how much I loved reading. Curling up with a good book instead of playing a game on my phone was my new nightly routine. How much I liked bubble baths, how had I not enjoyed these before? Some genius invented bath bombs during my quest to find my purpose! Where had they been all my life?! How good the new shampoo I bought smelled. I

Holly Cotton

remember how I couldn't lift my arms to shampoo my hair after my surgery, now I realized the importance of the aromatherapy. Letting it sit in my hair a little bit longer instead of rushing to go to the next mundane thing I had to do that day. How my kids talked to me. Instead of me telling them what to do, I realized they were little people who had fears and dreams just like me. I started listening to them. I realized it is a waste to let a good song play without singing along. Especially a good classic 80's song. If I am in the store and I hear a song I hit the notes with them. Will I be on my death bed sad that I sang in the store or will it be regret because I didn't loosen up and enjoy my life? These are some of my happy places. Things that make me happy to be alive and in the moment. Everyone has to find their own happy moment. What is it that you can do that makes your soul smile? That makes your strength shine bright? Do not be afraid of what others think of you. Believe me, none of those strangers will be there holding your hand if something happens to you. Why care about their opinion of you now? My purpose. To show people how lighthearted life can be! People constantly say "Holly, I love your energy". I think to myself, I don't have any energy, I am just living. I think if more people "just lived" they would have that same energy. Surround yourself with those with a purpose. Do not let your light be dimmed by a grumpy cat!

My doctor gives my number to patients that are recently diagnosed with cancer. Not just breast cancer. They have various types of lymphomas, leukemia, various organs. He said my outlook on life was uplifting and could benefit anyone trying to find a small glimpse of hope. I create a friendship with my fellow survivor network. They cry, I cry. We talk about the fears, the unknowns. The best thing is we talk about the things we do know. I learn about their families, pets, jobs. We talk about all the things that are important to us. It's amazing that every person I talked to has the same fear. That there is no time left. Death and sickness minutes are not like treadmill minutes that seem to go on forever. When you could lose your life you realize how much time you wasted. You realize all the things you want to do. No matter the person, the fear is always the same. So why is it so difficult for us to see this when we aren't sick? Why can't we see our purpose?

The very first person I spoke to was a breast cancer patient. She had been diagnosed two days before our conversation. Listening to her cry and tell her story made me remember all the details of my diagnosis again. I relived all of my fears as she discovered hers.

Holly Cotton

She was 40 and worked fulltime. She had two children. Same as me. She felt a lump as she was taking a shower. She had put off going to the doctor thinking it would go away. She said after a few months she realized she needed to go get tested and her diagnosis came after the usual pattern of tests. Her cancer was tipple negative. Without getting too technical "triple negative" means that when they dissect your cancer cells they see how they react to different substances to determine the course of treatment. Being triple negative means that the breast cancer does not respond to hormone therapy. I was triple positive. Meaning that my course of treatment could be a hormonal medication to inhibit estrogen production. So with her type of cancer the treatment needed to be more intense. Chemotherapy and radiation are often the course after surgery to remove the tumor. Triple negative breast cancer is also described as a more aggressive cancer and harder to treat. We talked about what her doctor had told her about surgery. We discussed reconstruction and what I experienced. I remember just sitting on the phone one evening listening to her cry about all of her regrets. Worrying about what she may not be able to do after surgery. Her concerns about how to work undergoing chemotherapy. As I listened to this stranger's event, I realized that everyone goes through the same thoughts.

STRONG.

The same regrets of not enough time. We all feel the guilt of things we did not do. We caught up recently and she is doing well. She had two courses of chemotherapy because the first round was not effective. She lost her hair which has now grown back. She had to have a major reconstruction process using her own skin from her back to rebuild her breast. As she detailed her trauma, I was so proud of her strength.

Another time, I spoke to a gentleman that had been diagnosed with prostate cancer. He detailed a story of having intestinal problems for a while and finally succumbing and going to the doctor. They tested him and found prostate cancer and a small section of colon cancer. I recall listening to him vent about being angry at himself for not going to the doctor sooner. He also had surgery and chemotherapy. They removed a section of his colon. He had a colostomy for a while, that is the bag that is attached to the outside of your body that collects your stool. They do this to allow the surgical area to heal. Some people can have it reversed. The surgeon would take the two ends of the dissected colon and reattach them. Some people keep the colostomy forever. He was fortunate to have his reconnected. We are Facebook friends. I watched the posted pictures show him being frail and sickly to gradually gaining more weight and his skin color looking peachy again. I have watched his children growing up. Their family time together. He told me the same thing as everyone else who faces something traumatic. That he will never let another second go by in life without being thankful he is alive. That is the theme for all who overcome something. It doesn't just have to be cancer, it can be anything. We are all awakened. We start appreciating life and the things that we may lose.

Every year around my Cancerversary I start reflecting on the year's events. All that I've done that year leading up to October 12th. All of the people who have impacted my life, who have I impacted? I think about the things that I walked away from because I refuse to let negativity come into my bubble. All of my friends and family are used to the new me. They see a strong woman, working, traveling, living life. My story of cancer is a distant memory. They forget about all that I went through. Not that they don't love me or weren't there with me, but when it isn't your battle you don't think about it. You go on with your life. So I use this time to remind myself and everyone else that I'm still here. I call, actually call my loved ones. I talk to them and tell them that I love them in case I haven't recently. I remember that I'm still here. You never regret doing something good. When you have nothing but time to look at your life and what you've done in it, you won't regret the times you did the right things. The times you did something positive. You will only regret that you didn't hear that person's voice one last time, or give them a hug. Not everyone in your life is meant to be there. I ended some friendships because of my new outlook. I became distant to those who continued in their same place. I could no longer be around negative people. I could not continue relationships with people that were okay with staying in the same place. I needed to expand on my new found outlook on life. That's part of the growing process. Just like as you grow from a child to an adult. You can't fit into the same clothes that you did the year prior. So quit forcing yourself to fit in the environment you were before. It is okay to grow. It is okay to shed the dead layers of friendship that bring you nothing good. I have made closer friendships with strangers at this point in my life than people who I have known since childhood. Not everyone wants to walk down your path with you. Don't stop your self-discovery for them. You are responsible for your own happiness and your own purpose.

The funny thing about meeting all of these people was that I was put into the equation to help them. I was supposed to be a positive addition in their dark times. It was a two way street. Their struggles made me a better person. Their despair reopened my eyes to visualize my

Holly Cotton

blessings. The bonds that were created made me appreciate friendship. They reminded me that you can never have too many positive people in your life. Bad relationships? Drop them like dead weight, but keep those people that warm your soul close by. There will always be days you feel grumpy and ungrateful. You must stop and remind yourself how blessed you are. If you can see your kids making a mess or the dog digging up your new plant, reflect on those that are blind. Hear your children arguing or their music is up too loud, reflect on being deaf. Yes, I still want to throat punch my kids on a daily basis, but then I stop and remember my purpose. Remember that I am still here to live and love.

Chapter Nine:

So I'm Strong...

Over the last year I have focused on being strong in all avenues of my life. I am the strongest I have ever been in my life, both physically and mentally. I created a social media group that acts as a support group. My followers and friends love seeing me flip a huge tractor tire I keep in my garage. I don't do this for them I do it for me. When I don't feel like getting out of bed and

Holly Cotton

going to the gym, I remember those days I couldn't. I remember those days I couldn't drive. The days I couldn't raise up a gallon of milk. Now here I am flipping a three hundred pound tire. Now of course my definition of strong is just that. MY DEFINITION. Everyone must find their own purpose. Their own motivation. Mine is that I made that vow after surgery that I wouldn't stay weak. I had grown so much emotionally, why not grow physically too. I began going to the gym every day. I put down the five pound weights and grabbed the twenty pound weights. I remember the sense of accomplishment when I began getting stronger. Struggling to do five repetitions of an exercise and then progressing to do ten. The satisfaction of going up in weight. I began to work out with some men in the gym to challenge myself even more. I got my fitness certification so that I could train others to do the same. To feel the same satisfaction when their clothes fit better. When they lifted more weight. Or when they were able to do exercises they couldn't do before. Again, my purpose. Helping others find their strength.

The other day I got a very long message from a previous coworker about having a hysterectomy. She said that she had uterine cancer so they chose to do a course of radiation to her abdomen after surgery. She wrote about how she was feeling mentally exhausted from the

84

fears and unknowns. We went back and forth for several days. On one of her messages she told me that a post I put up using water bottles to create a workout routine made her day. She said she was always so scared to go into the gym. Unsure of the machines and technology that surrounded her. She was worried about how to jump start her workouts to get back into shape without overstraining herself. After she saw that video she grabbed two water bottles and began working out. Following all the exercises I recorded. I remember when I recorded the video I thought no one would watch it or try the exercises. Someone actually needed that two minute video to change their life.

I have had numerous breast cancer survivors reach out to me. They are at various stages of their diagnoses and treatments. I always get the same themed message. Thanking me for showing there is life after cancer. That they have something to look for after surgery. That the weakness you feel eventually goes away. I reply to each and every person's message with optimism. Most of the time you feel so helpless and unsure of your future. I know firsthand, I went through the same things. Thinking you will never get past this trauma. I am so grateful I can use my tragedy to give others hope. Just the other day I got a message from a breast cancer survivor telling me that she had set three goals to achieve in the next year. She wanted to run a mud race just like me and two other things. I was so amazed! "Just like you" was the phrase she used. I told her it is a common feeling amongst survivors after cancer. You refuse to be limited by anything ever again! She is going to let me know when she competes and I am going to be on that sideline cheering her on when she crosses that finish line. Strong is more than just muscles. It is being able to overcome whatever challenge you need to in order to come out stronger on the other side.

With the discovery of being strong however, comes backlash. With me being strong, people doubted the severity of my cancer journey. How is she doing all of this workout stuff if she had breast cancer? They forget that illness is often temporary. I was still Holly, not just Holly with breast cancer. Yes, I had survived my battle. Many other people have not. Breast cancer was something that I overcame; it was not all that I was. I received messages from people telling me to "quit showing off" and that I must have not really been sick. I remember one received message that told me to quit using breast cancer as an excuse. He went on to say that if I was really so hurt after cancer I would look hurt. I would have shown my scars. He told me to quit giving people false hope about life after cancer. I was appalled. How could someone even think this about me? I had a double mastectomy! I had gone through all I did and someone would now think I was making up my story? I did reply back to this person with a very long paragraph including several exclamation points. I referenced several celebrities who look "just fine" and have not let cancer stop them from accomplishing any of their goals. Thousands of woman display their strength mentally and physically. They offer spiritual centering and support to ensure the soul is healed, not just the body. So I began to shy away from being so strong. I didn't want people to be scared by my strength. I didn't want women to think I was showing off because I was strong. I thought about what I needed to do. How do I fulfil my purpose without being over the top? Then, the epiphany. Why would I ever want to buffer my shine? Why do we feel guilty and ashamed about being great? Being strong is an awesome thing! Being strong was sexy!! It made me who I was. I am going to show the world that after all you go through in life, it only adds to your beauty. To the sexiness that defines your character. The scars that make you sexy and beautiful. Not just physical scars, but those sad stories. Those emotional scars. The events in life that thought they could break you, yet you came out on the other side like a champion. Anything that happened in your life that requires an ounce of strength. I decided to combine being strong with being sexy no matter who thought negatively about it. I wanted to make the phrase my own, so I decided to replace the "y" with an "i". Because "I" was sexi! I began using the phrase with my workouts and anything else that I did. Sexy comes from so many outlets. Not just physically.

So here we are now. The development of Strong Squad. I knew that "strong" was always my go to word. With all I have been through, how could I even consider another word? I began a group for my friends where we could gather and be strong together. I constantly explain that being strong is defined by your own measurements. Don't compare yourself to anyone else, ever. I learned from my battles that there is no one more awesome than me. How can you demand love if you don't love yourself? How can you feel strong if you're constantly breaking your own self down? That is exactly what happens when you compare yourself to others. When I hear someone say "I want to look like you", or "I want a __ like so and so" I jump out of my skin. You do not want to be like me. You want to be the best you that you can be. Life is just that simple. If we could all embrace our own accomplishments and the circumstances we are faced with instead of always wanting more, or thinking something is better. We could be so much happier. Don't let a traumatic event